I'm Saved, Now What?

A Must Have Manual for Every New Convert

Author: Dr. Barbara D. Eason
Edited by: Dr. LaHoma A. Wellman
My Father's House Ministries, Inc.

AuthorHouse™
1663 Liberty Drive
Bloomington, IN 47403
www.authorhouse.com
Phone: 1-800-839-8640

© 2010 Dr. Barbara Eason. All rights reserved.

No part of this book may be reproduced, stored in a retrieval system, or transmitted by any means without the written permission of the author.

First published by AuthorHouse   5/20/2010

ISBN: 978-1-4520-2734-0 (sc)

Library of Congress Control Number: 2010907220

Printed in the United States of America
Bloomington, Indiana

This book is printed on acid-free paper.

Dedication

This book is dedicated to the members of My Father's House Ministries, Inc., because I am thankful for all of your love, support, and encouragement, and for allowing me to be your overseer. I always remember that there is no "me without you," and no "us without we." You have hung in there with me from the beginning. Special mention to our very first deacon, Angela Shanetta King-Swift, and our current head deacon, Moses Brisbon, for keeping things in top-notch order.

To my goddaughter, Tyonna J. Winfree, I can't imagine me without you. Godmommy loves you with an endless love.

To my sisters, Jackie, Maggie, LaHoma, Lesleigh, Julia, Ismaillah, Texanna, Julianna, and Helene (my Swedish sister); my sister-in-law, Veva; and my favorite brother, Franklin, I am so truly blessed to have such a large and loving support team. If you can't count on family to buy your book, who can you count on (lol)!

To my mother, Mrs. Martha Lucille Eason, what a great mother you are. Guess you didn't do such a bad job bringing us up after all. Where would we be without you? I love you with all my heart. To my other mother, Mrs. Linda Cooper, in Guyana, South America—who takes really good care of me when I am there—thanks for all that you do. I love you so much.

To my best and dearest friend, my prayer partner, confidante, the person who knows all my secrets and will carry them to her grave, Elder Linda M. Eddings. Everyone should have a friend like you. A priceless gift from God. I don't think you will ever know how much I appreciate you.

To all of my nieces and nephews, great-nieces and great-nephews, and my cousin Susie Williams, I am blessed and fortunate to have each of you in my life. I am so proud of what God is doing in and through you, and I pray that each of you will continue to submit and surrender completely to His perfect and divine will. And to those who are not submitting, don't worry; with all the prayers that are out, you will.

To Mark Hooper, what do I say? My forever friend, my soul mate. I thank God for placing you in my life. You are a great sounding board, relentless prayer partner, and huge supporter. Thanks for challenging me and for the boldness to tell me the truth when I am wrong, which is *so* not often.

To Dr. Mary-Ann Odems, pastor of the Lion of Judah Covenant Ministries in Geneva, Switzerland, my identical twin in the spirit, I love you and thank God for you.

To Reverend Monica Robertson, a true friend indeed and a gift from God, thanks for allowing God to use you to make this possible. I am blessed to have you as a sister in Christ and as a friend.

To Pastor Viola Barner, I am where I am today because you had the courage to correct me when I was wrong, the wisdom to guide and encourage me when I felt like giving up, the strength to push me beyond what my flesh was feeling, and a life that taught me how to work the word of faith. What a mighty woman of God you are. You are priceless, and I love you with all of my heart.

And last but not least, to God the Father in creation, the Son in redemption, and the Holy Ghost in the church, I am nothing without you. Thanks for inspiring me to write this book to reach the nations. What an awesome God you are! Don't ever let your Holy Spirit depart from me, because without you I am nothing.

Special Mention

Dr. LaHoma Anne Eason-Wellman has been instrumental to me in so many ways. First, she is my sister by birth, a priceless gift from God, an earthly treasure, an individual in whom I delight to and honor to call friend. I feel that I was granted a double blessing because she is also my sister in Christ, because we are both born-again believers.

When you are an overseer and have churches located in the United States and abroad and operate under an evangelistic anointing as well, you have to have a rock at home who is strong in the Lord, strong in faith, can carry the ministry, and from whom you can draw strength. That individual has to be dependable, and you have to know that he or she is going to be there for the long haul, no matter what. I have found that in Dr. Eason-Wellman.

She is the senior pastor of My Father's House Ministries, Inc., in our headquarters church located in Richmond, Virginia. Because of her love for God, commitment to His service, and dedication to living a holy life and bringing God's people the Bible's way, I am afforded the opportunity to do what I have a passion for, and that is to go forth and preach the gospel to the nations of the world.

This woman of God faithfully stands in the gap and labors with the children of God without asking for anything in return, fulfilling the call of, "outreach in our own backyard," for which she has a passion. She is a treasure to the ministry.

Dr. Eason-Wellman coauthored this book. Her knowledge of the Word of God, her research, her spiritual advice, and her patience in working with me are to be commended. There is not a time that I need her that she does not make herself available.

Just in case I haven't told you this lately, I loved you yesterday, I love you today, I will love you tomorrow. I appreciate you to the utmost. We make an awesome team, don't cha think?

Contents

Foreword — xi

Chapter I: The New Birth Experience — 1

Chapter II: What Comes Next? — 11

Chapter III: Maintaining a Personal and Intimate Relationship with Jesus Christ — 19

Chapter IV: Holiness—It's What God Requires — 29

Chapter V: Questions Frequently Asked by New Converts — 35

Definitions — 43

Closing Remarks — 47

Foreword

Praise the Lord and congratulations! You have just made the most important decision of your life! You have taken the first step toward eternal life with our Creator. By confessing Jesus Christ as Lord ("If you shall confess with your mouth, the Lord Jesus, and shall believe in your heart that God hath raised Him from the dead, you shall be saved" [Romans 10:19]), and by inviting Him into your heart ("'Behold, I stand at the door and knock, if any man hear my voice, and open the door, I will come in …'" [Revelation 3:20]), you are about to embark on the most amazing experience of your lifetime.

The foundation of any ministry, whether it is your local ministry or the personal ministry that you are birthed into, should be built on the foundation of the Lord Jesus Christ, which is the Word made flesh (John 1:14), who is the Rock (I Corinthians 6:4), who is the Chief Cornerstone (Isaiah 28:16; I Peter 2:6), who is the Foundation (I Corinthians 3:11), who is the Head Cornerstone (Matthew 21:42; Acts 4:11).

The Bible warns us that in the last days, many false teachers will arise, and because of this, many believers will give heed to false doctrines. Although these false teachers will spread lies, distort the truth, dilute the Word of God, and simply say that God's Holy Word no longer applies, we, as God's elect, must remember that no matter how many people follow the liars, the solid foundation of God's truth *never* changes. It is never shaken and will never fade or fail. As long as we follow God's truth, He will never forsake us!

When I first got converted, I didn't fully understand what salvation was all about. The church I attended did not have new members' classes. I had lots of questions about the Word of God, but when I asked those questions, I felt really bad, because I was made to feel as though I was being rebellious or questioning the authority of the leaders. We were told what to do and how to do it. If we didn't, we were labeled as disobedient to the faith, so we just simply followed instructions.

Years later, I found that many scriptures from the Bible had been misquoted or rephrased to the benefit of the pastor, and some of the things that were being taught at the church were not even biblical. So, it's going to be very important for you to study the Word of God.

The new birth experience and your walk with the Lord Jesus Christ are beautiful. When you seek to know the Lord and not just merely know *about* Him, you will find yourself entering into a personal relationship and falling more and more in love with your Creator. More than that, you will find joy in fellowshipping with your Savior. You will learn to know His voice, and you will eagerly answer when He speaks to you. He will reveal Himself to you in many manifestations. And you will long to have His presence (the essence of His Being) and not just simply the presents (the gifts) with which He will bless you.

I cannot stress enough that the new birth experience *does not* eliminate hardships in your life. It is important for you to understand that when you got born again, you did not lose your old nature, you just got a new nature; thus, it will help you to understand how to keep the old nature from dominating in your life. Having Jesus living inside of you makes this transition into your new life so much easier. I often tell the members of My Father's House Ministries, Inc., "It's hard making it with Jesus, but it is impossible to make it without Him."

This manual contains biblical information to help you understand what is expected of you. It will provide answers to some of the most frequently asked questions. The following chapters will explain the conversion that took place in your life, the importance of the infilling of the Holy Ghost, why water baptism is necessary, what it means to renew your mind, how to maintain your personal and intimate relationship with Jesus Christ, why forgiveness is so essential to the Christian life, and so much more!

As you begin to grow in your Christian faith and walk with Christ, you will begin to experience various seasons in your life. Don't let this frighten you. You will have the leaders from your local church to walk you through each process as you encounter them.

You may be asking yourself, "What does seasons have to do with my life?" Ecclesiastes 3:1 says, "To everything there is a season and a time to every purpose under the heaven." During the first years of my life, I lived on a farm. I know firsthand all to well the importance of changing seasons, especially as my mother used to work in the tobacco fields, and my older sisters and cousins used to pick cucumbers. My sister Maggie and I could hardly wait until harvest was over, so we could go glean the corn that was left behind in the fields to have spending money for the weekends. With each season came what seemed like overwhelming tasks that were necessary for the productiveness of the next. Had the farmer been lazy, careless, or miscalculated his timing, he could have lost his entire harvest for that year. He would not have been the only one affected by the loss: those who depended on him for jobs, the retailers who purchased the products he produced, and the animals that relied on food from those same crops would also be affected. As it is with our Christian lives. When we don't endure our seasons, our failures don't just affect us but those who are surrounded by us as well.

Without the changing seasons in your life, you cannot be fruitful or productive for the Kingdom of God. Each season that comes offers something that is necessary for continued growth in your walk with Christ. There will be times when it will seem like your seasons will never end. There will be other times when you will never want your seasons to end. At My Father's House Ministries, Inc., all the members love spring, autumn, and winter. They never want them to end. When one rejoices, we all rejoice. Oh, but during their summer seasons, my phone never stops ringing. It's constantly one trial after another. Everything is an emergency, and the prayer wheel turns nonstop.

Spring will come, with its gentle, rain-filled days that will stimulate growth in your spiritual walk with Christ. You will feel exhilarated and carefree. You will sense the presence of God. You will know that He is holding your hand and guiding your every stop. It is during this season that new and old converts alike have a tendency to become complacent. You must continue to grow, seek God, read your Bible, fast, and pray.

Summer is the most dreaded season. It is long and hot. There will be times when it appears that the season will never end. It is during this season that you must be extremely careful. It is here that many Christians fall away, because they can't endure the heat of summer.

During this season, there is nothing to attract you, or distract you. You may not sense the presence of God; you just have to trust that He is there. You have to endure.

Autumn comes and brings with it an abundant harvest for those who have sown diligently, endured the heat of the summer, and waited patiently on the Lord. It is the time of rejoicing, for the blessings of the Lord are pouring in!

Here comes winter, that long-awaited season where God gives you the rest that you need so that He can start the process all over again.

As you read these pages, allow the Holy Spirit to minister to your heart. As with any material that you study, it is important to always have your Bible (I recommend the King James Version) open so that you can verify the accuracy of the scriptures that are used in the text.

You are encouraged to read your Bible and pray every day. In doing so, the Holy Spirit will enlighten you, and your relationship with the Savior will be strengthened. As you read, you will find that the Word of God is exciting. It comes alive on the pages and gives you life. You will see the lives of ordinary men and women who did great things simply because they trusted in the living God.

Romans 13:11–14 says, "And that, knowing the time, that now it is high time to awake out of sleep; for now is our salvation nearer than when we believed. The night is far spent, the day is at hand; let us therefore cast off the works of darkness and let us put on the armor of light. Let us walk honestly as in the day; not in rioting and drunkenness, not in chambering and wantonness, not in strife and envying. But put ye on the Lord Jesus Christ, and make not provisions for the flesh to fulfill the lust thereof." For this reason, more so now than ever before, it is extremely urgent that born-again believers fully commit their ways to the Lord Jesus Christ and allow Him to direct their paths.

Don't be afraid to ask your local leaders questions concerning anything you don't understand. They are there to serve you.

At the end of each chapter, you will have the opportunity to write a brief summary of what you gained from each chapter.

My prayer is that this manual will be a useful tool as you make your transition and continue to go forward in the plans that God has for you.

Chapter I:
The New Birth Experience

- **Generate Man**—Created in the image of God and placed in a perfect environment. God said in Genesis 1:26 (KJV), "Let us make man in our image, after our likeness."
- **Degenerate Man**—Fallen from grace, sin entered and a spiritual death took place. "The Lord God commanded the man, saying, 'Of every tree of the garden thou mayest freely eat, but of the tree of the knowledge of good and evil, thou shalt not eat of it for in the day that thou eatest thereof, thou shalt surely die'" (Genesis 2:16–17 KJV).
- **Regenerate Man**—Sinful man needed a way back to God. By accepting Jesus Christ as the atonement for your sin, asking Him to come into your heart and reign over your life, He became the bridge that connected you back to God the Father. "But this one man, after he had offered one sacrifice for sins, forever sat down on the right hand of God: From henceforth expecting till his enemies be made his footstool. For by one offering He hath perfected forever them that are sanctified (Hebrews 10:12–14 KJV). "That if thou shalt confess with thy mouth the Lord Jesus and shalt believe in thine heart that God hath raised Him from the dead, thou shalt be saved" (Romans 10:9 KJV).

The Holy Spirit inspired me to write this manual to assist you in making the transition from your old way of life into your new walk with Jesus Christ. Those of you who read this manual will find that the answers to

1

your questions are simple and easy to understand, and they can be found in your King James Version of the Holy Bible. You are encouraged to search the Holy Scriptures daily, because in them, you have life.

How Did I Become a Sinner?

That is one of the first questions asked by most new converts. They believe that they are morally good if they don't use vile language, smoke, use drugs, drink alcohol, commit fornication or adultery, or lie, among other things, and that they are not in danger of going to hell. That is one of the biggest misconceptions dispatched by Satan. And if the truth is not made known, they die and go to an everlasting, ever-burning lake of fire (Revelation 21:14).

The good news is that sin did not start with you. It started with Adam and Eve. Man was created perfect in the image of God. Unlike nature and the universe, which was created to obey God's every command, man was given the seed of choice, thus a free will. This is known as *generate man*. Along with the free will that was given to man came some specific instructions. Genesis 2:16–17, "And the Lord God commanded the man, saying, 'Of every tree of the garden thou mayest freely eat, but of the tree of the knowledge of good and evil, thou shalt not eat of it for in the day that thou eatest thereof, thou shalt surely die.'" Sin brought separation (spiritual death) between a holy God and His creation.

Genesis 3:6–7 reads, "And when the woman saw that the tree was good for food, and that it was pleasant to the eyes, and a tree to be desired to make one wise, she took of the fruit thereof, and did eat, and gave also unto her husband with her and he did eat. And the eyes of them both were opened, and they knew that they were naked." This is known as *degenerate man*. He had deliberately chosen to disobey the direct command from God, and thus, fellowship with God was broken.

Because of this act of disobedience by Adam and Eve, we were all born into sin. "Behold, I was shaped in iniquity, and in sin did my mother conceive me" (Psalm 51:5). So no matter how earthly good we were, "We are all as an unclean thing, and all our righteousness are as filthy rags" (Isaiah 64:6 KJV). Because of this, we were all in desperate need of redemption. We needed a savior to put us back in right standing with God, to repair the broken breach, or pay the sin debt created by Adam and Eve. Jesus would bridge the gap between the Holy God and unholy humanity. We needed salvation.

What Is Salvation, and Why Do I Need It?

Salvation is the saving of a person from sin or its consequences in the life after death; saving from danger or evil (Webster's New World College Dictionary, 5th ed., p. 463). In Hebrew, it is deliverance, victory, help, health, liberty, prosperity, and safety (Strong's, *Strongest Concordance*, p. 38). In Greek, it is translated to mean defender or defense, rescuer or safety; Christ or God (Strong's, p. 88).

You need salvation because Satan is deceiving people into believing that they can have salvation apart from Jesus Christ. His method is to make them think that as long as they have good moral values, they are okay. His concept is this: "I'm a relatively good person. I don't hurt nobody. I live a better life than some of the people going to church. I don't drink or smoke. I don't have sex outside of marriage. Like I say, I'm a good person." Wrong! It does not matter how good you *think* you are living. There is absolutely no salvation without Jesus Christ. The Bible clearly tells us in Hebrews 9:22 (KJV), "Without the shedding of blood there is no remission of sin." Good morals and values do not get you into heaven; Jesus Christ is the only ticket to heaven. In John 14:6 (KJV), it says, "Jesus said unto them, 'I am the Way, the Truth, and the Life; No man cometh unto the Father but by Me.'" Therefore, contrary to anything else that is taught, there is no other way to heaven except through the Man, Jesus Christ!

Because we were born into sin, and no matter how earthly good we are, without the blood atonement of Jesus Christ and His imputed righteousness, our righteousness just doesn't measure up. The Bible is very clear about that, "Our righteousness is a filthy rags" (Isaiah 64:6). Romans 3:23 tells us, "We have all sinned and come short of the glory of God." But don't feel bad; it had nothing to do with you. Remember, it started with Adam and Eve, back in the Garden of Eden. That is why we need salvation to restore us into a right relationship with God. And the only way to do that is to confess the Lord Jesus Christ with your mouth and believe in your heart that God raised Him from the dead. There is no other way to get back to God. Remember what you just read: Jesus said, "'I am the Way, the Truth, and the Life; and no man cometh unto the Father but by Me'" (John 14:6).

How Do I Get Saved or Accept Jesus Christ as My Personal Lord and Savior?

It's simple. The Bible tells us in Romans 10:9, "If thou shall confess with thy mouth the Lord Jesus and shalt believe in thine heart that God hath raised Him from the dead, thou shalt be saved." Revelation 3:20 says, "Behold, I stand at the door and knock, If any man hears me calling him and opens the door, I will come in and fellowship with him and he with Me." Ephesians 2:8 says, "For by grace are we saved through faith." It's just that simple.

So once you acknowledge that you are a sinner, make your confession, open the door of your heart and invite Jesus Christ to come into your heart, you are saved! And the purpose of this book is to let you know that it does not end at the altar! It is just the beginning of your newfound relationship with God the Father. Dr. Eason-Wellman and I encourage you to surround yourself with other born-again believers who are strong in the Lord and chasing hard after God. This is so important to recent converts. Be sure to attend your local Bible study and worship services.

Remember, being born again does not free us from trials or tests. Satan will launch attacks against you now more than ever, because you are now out of his grasp and he wants to get you back. So stay prayerful and read your Bible every day!

The Penalty of Sin

In Romans 6:23, Paul clearly states, "The wages of sin is death." Wages are what you receive for the work that you do. In this case, it refers to the works of the flesh. Galatians 5:19–21 gives us a vivid list: "'Now the <u>works of the flesh</u> are adultery, fornication, uncleanness, lasciviousness, idolatry, witchcraft, hatred, variance, emulations, wrath, strife, seditions, heresies, envying, murders, drunkenness, reveling, and such like of the which I tell you before, as I have also told you in time past, that they which do such things <u>shall not inherit the kingdom of God</u>. These works will keep you spiritually dead and cause you to be separated from God if you do not overcome them.'"

The apostle Paul reminds us in his second letter to Timothy 2:19, "Let everyone that names the name of Christ, depart from iniquity." It is possible to remove yourself from sinful situations. Romans 6:14 lets us know, "Sin shall not have dominion [power] over you." As you continue your walk with Christ, and your fellowship with Him increases, you will notice that you will have less desire for the things that are contrary to His will. Your utmost desire will be to be found in His presence, pleasing Him.

For those who continue to walk in the ways of sinful and lustful desires, the book of Revelation declares in 21:8, "But the fearful, and unbelieving, and the abominable, and the murderers, and whoremongers, and sorcerers, idolaters, and all liars shall have their part in the lake which burns with fire and brimstone, which is the second death."

I encourage all new converts to be diligent in attending Bible study, prayer meetings, and Sunday morning worship services. Surround yourself with people who love God and are seeking to go higher in Him. Don't be found in groups filled with gossip, talebearing, and lots of foolishness. These things will hinder your spiritual growth. Dare to be different.

One of Satan's main strategies is to keep you busy. He doesn't even care if you go to church as long as you are so tired when you get to church you are unable to pay attention. It's okay to be involved in activities with your local church, but don't get so bogged down with activities and forget to reserve personal, alone time with the Lord Jesus Christ. Just as you make hair, nail, and doctor appointments, make appointments to be with Jesus, to study your word, and to have intercessory prayer. I can tell you from experience, it is so easy to get caught up in the hustle and bustle of the day and omit praying and spending time alone with Jesus! I've been there. And if you miss one service, whether it is Bible study, worship service, or prayer, Satan will give you a thousand reasons why you should miss another and another and another.

Every step of the way, he is going to tell you that you made a mistake in choosing to serve God. He's going to tell you that it doesn't take that much fasting and praying. He's going to say you are too young or too old to serve God. He is going to say you still have time. He is going to say serving God is boring. He is going to tell you not to tithe and give offerings to your local church. He is going to make accusations against your brothers and sisters in Christ. None of his strategies are new: he uses the same ones against everybody. His plan is to divide and conquer. He is going to try relentlessly to win you back. Don't listen to him, because he is a deceiver. Revelation 20:10 says, "And the devil that deceived them was cast into the lake of fire and brimstone ... and shall be tormented day and night for ever and ever." John 8:44 says, "Ye are of your father the devil ... he was a murderer from the beginning ... and he abode not in the truth because there is no truth in him. When he speak a lie, he speak of his own, for he is a liar and the father of it." So you see, anything the devil tells you is a lie. He will *never* tell you the truth, because he can't. Did you notice how Jesus is total truth and Satan is a total liar? They are extreme opposites.

Your Responsibility Toward God

Your responsibility toward God is found in Romans 12:1–2, "I beseech [plead with you] therefore brethren, by the mercies of God, that ye present your bodies a living sacrifice, holy, and acceptable unto God which is your reasonable service. And be not conformed to this world, but be ye transformed by the *renewing of your mind*, that you may prove what is that good and acceptable and perfect will of God."

You may ask, "What does it mean to present my body as a living sacrifice unto the Lord? I thought Jesus died and became the sacrifice for us." That's true. Jesus did become the sacrificial Lamb for us, to redeem us from the curse of the law (Genesis 3:13–14). However, as Christians, we become partakers of his suffering, and it is our duty as ambassadors for Christ (II Corinthians 5:20) to live a life of total surrender and self-denial. You must die to things of the world in order for Christ to be seen in and through us. "I am crucified with Christ, nevertheless I live; yet not I but Christ liveth in me" (Galatians 2:20). There will be things from your old nature that will try to draw you back to your old lifestyle, but you must hold fast to the Word of God and remember that you are a new creature in Christ Jesus! Your body is now the temple of God Most High.

Hebrews 10:1–14 reveals how Jesus gave Himself willingly for us. A sacrifice comes with a price; it always costs you something. Salvation is a free gift, but to manifest the pure anointing of God, you must pay by living a life sold out to Jesus Christ. Therefore, it is imperative that each individual count the cost before they take on the name of Jesus.

What Does It Mean to Renew My Mind, and How Is It Done?

Renew means to do over again or bring back to a good condition. It also means to begin again. This subject is very dear to me and close to my heart. It is one of the primary reasons this book was written. When I first started to pastor, I had a lot to learn. I would study the Word of God for hours on end. Sunday mornings would come, and I would go to church and preach what I thought was a "good word." I would prepare the Bible study lessons, assuming they were plain and simple and anyone could understand them because I could.

One Sunday, after I had preached on renewing the mind, one of my nephews, Shannon, who is also a member of the church, came to me and said, "Pastor, I don't have a problem with renewing my mind, but I don't know how." I said, "But I just got finished ministering on the subject. What do you mean you don't understand?" He said, "You told us that we needed to renew our minds, and that we needed to do it on a daily basis, but you never told us *how* to renew our minds." That got my attention! I realized that as leaders, we have a responsibility to ensure that the Word of God is plain and simple, so that *everyone* understands what we are talking about. We are never to *assume* anything when it comes to people's souls.

This is the illustration I use to explain what it means to renew your mind. Almost everyone knows what a cassette tape is. So, we start with a blank tape. Before we were converted, we recorded secular music on that tape. We enjoyed listening to R&B, hip-hop, and jazz. Now we have been introduced to Jesus Christ. His Word tells us to be holy and not conform to the things of this world. So, we put the tape into the cassette recorder, hit the rewind button, and on that same tape, we record gospel, praise, and worship music. We just renewed the tape. We have the same tape; we are just listening to different music on it.

Renewing your mind is accomplished pretty much in the same way. Before conversion, you watched certain things on television, you may have read certain kinds of books, engaged in certain types of conversations, went to clubs, listened to worldly music, and participated in other worldly activities and things that are contrary to the Word of God. When you gave your life to Christ, you change the way you walk, talk, act, and think. Why? Because I Corinthians 10:21 says, "You can not drink of the Lord's cup and the cup of devils, you can not be partakers of the Lord's table and the table of devils." Solomon tells us in Proverbs 23:7, "As a man thinks in his heart, so is he."

And last, we have the example of Moses. He was raised in Pharaoh's house. He had privilege and authority. But he also had compassion for his Jewish family. He fled from Egypt after killing an Egyptian for beating one of the Jews. While he was there, God visited him, telling him he was to be the deliverer of the Jews.

Although Moses had to right to be called the son of Pharaoh's daughter and live a life of luxury, he refused it and chose to do it God's way, rather than enjoy the pleasures and status of sin.

If you want to be renewed, you have to make up your mind that regardless of who or what comes or goes, you are going to serve the Lord. Your attitude must be, "I would rather get it all from God and nothing from man," and you have to stick to it. You may have to wait longer for it, but I can testify that it will be well worth the wait.

When you decide that you are going to renew your mind and follow God, you will have to go against the wind and the way of the crowd. Salvation is a free gift, but to have the anointing of God is going to cost you something.

Having the Mind of Christ

That's saying a lot. Right now, you must be wondering how in the world you're supposed to know the mind of Christ while still trying to figure out all this other stuff. Don't panic! Jesus had a mind to do the will of the Father (Hebrews 10:9): "Then said he, 'Lo, I come to do thy will, O God.'" He knew what His purpose was and never lost focus of it. His purpose on earth was:

- To Overcome the World—John 16:33: "In the world ye shall have tribulation, but be of good cheer, I have *overcome the world*."
- To Condemn Sin in the Flesh—Romans 8:3: "For what the law could not do, in that it was weak through the flesh, God

sending his own Son in the likeness of *sinful flesh, and for sin, condemned sin in the flesh.*"

- To Destroy the Works of the Devil—I John 3:8: "For this purpose the Son of God was manifested, that *He might destroy the works of the devil.*"

Jesus had a mind to be obedient, even unto death. He did not think it robbery to be equal with God. He did not come seeking to be served; instead, he came with a mind to serve others. He was not looking for a reputation or glory for himself. He was looking to glorify God in all aspects of His life.

So, to have the mind of Christ, you must seek and know the will of the Father for your life. You must not lose focus of your purpose. Don't get distracted by petty things that have no bearing on your eternal being. Practice living holy, serving others, seeking God, living peaceably with all men. When you make a mistake, be quick to repent. Above all, keep your mind stayed on Jesus, because Isaiah 26:3 says, "'I will keep you in perfect peace if your mind is stayed on me, because you trust in me.'"

The New Birth Translation

The new birth translation means to be moved from one position or place to another. Colossians 1:12–14 says, "Giving thanks unto the Father, which hath made us meet to be partakers of the inheritance of the saints in light' who hat delivered us from the power of darkness and hath *translated* us into the kingdom of His dear Son; in whom we have redemption through His blood, even the forgiveness of sins." Hallelujah! What does all of this mean? Paul is simply saying, "Always be thankful to the Father who have made you fit to share all the wonderful things that belong to those who live in the kingdom of light. For God has rescued you out of the darkness and gloom of Satan's kingdom and positioned you into the kingdom of His dear Son, Jesus Christ, who bought your freedom with His own blood and forgave all your sins!"

As you continue this new birth translation, glean as much as you can from your leaders. All too often, new converts are anxious to get placed in leadership positions. But with leadership comes lots of responsibility. You may see the ushers serving at the doors of the church, or the deacons fulfilling their duties diligently, but if they came the Bible's way, they did not get there overnight. Dr. Eason-Wellman and I agree that it is best first to develop your Christian characteristics. As you attend your local Bible study and worship services, and as you study the Word of God, you will find these characteristics are very necessary. They are called the beatitudes. I call them the attitude of Christ. You will also learn the fruit of the Spirit. These attributes will help you conduct yourself as one who has taken on the nature of Christ in the most trying of circumstances.

It takes a lot of discipline to become a good leader, and one of the first qualities of being a good leader is to be a good follower; the second is to be a good server. The character of Christ must be evident in every aspect of your worship. There will be times when you will find that you will have to press to read the Word of God. You must, therefore, train your body and mind to do what it should do and not what it wants to do. Always seek to please God. Be faithful, and always let your service be unto God and not unto man.

Chapter II:
What Comes Next?

But ye shall receive power, after that the Holy Ghost is
come upon you; and ye shall be witnesses unto me here
in Jerusalem and in all Judea and in Samaria and unto
the uttermost part of the earth. (Acts 1:8)

The Importance of the Infilling of the Holy Ghost

The verse you just read lets you that the Holy Ghost equips us for
ministry. Jesus's last recorded words have come to be known as the
"Great Commission." In the book of Acts, Luke writes about men and
women who took that commission seriously and began to spread the
news of a risen Savior to the most remote corners of the world. Before
they began their great mission, however, Jesus commanded them to wait
in Jerusalem until they were filled with the Holy Ghost that God the
Father had promised them.

The same reason it was important for them to receive the Holy
Ghost back then is the same reason you should strive to receive the
Holy Ghost today. It is that part of Christ within us that gives you
overcoming power. I John 4:4 says, "Because greater is he that is within
you, than he that is in the world." Jesus told the disciples, "'When the
Holy Ghost has come upon you, you will receive power to testify about
me with great effect, to the people to the ends of the earth about his
death, burial and resurrection'" (Acts 1:8).

Regardless of what people tell you about the Holy Ghost/Holy
Spirit, it is needful in this day and time. In order to walk holy, you must
receive the Holy Ghost. Jesus thought it was necessary back then, thus it

must still be necessary today. It is what teaches us and brings all things to our remembrance. John 14:26 says, "'But the Comforter, which is the Holy Ghost, whom the Father will send in my name, He shall teach you all things and bring all things to your remembrance whatsoever I have said to you.'"

The Holy Ghost is necessary if you want the power of God demonstrated in your life. It is there not just as the Comforter to bring you comfort when it seems that all the world is against you, it is there also to equip you with power, "But ye shall receive power after that the Holy Ghost is come upon you" (Acts 1:8).

The power of God that will come upon you will cause the desires that you used to have to cease to be of importance to you. Once you take on His nature, you will no longer want to go to the same places you used to go. With the aid of the Holy Ghost, you will no longer have a desire to fornicate, drink alcohol, smoke, curse, chase men or women, or commit other sins. Your desire will be to please God the Father. You will find that you are, indeed, a new creation in Christ, and you will come to realize that you are incomplete without Him.

Once you are empowered with the Holy Ghost, you will realize that you are *in* the world but not *of* the world. No one will have to tell you to change your friends, because when you begin to witness to them about Christ, they will automatically distance themselves from you. You will find yourself with new friends who desire the same thing you desire: more of Christ, "Therefore, if any man be in Christ, he is a new creature; old things are passed away; behold all things are become new" (II Corinthians 5:16).

So, the infilling of the Holy Ghost is important in your life because it makes you an effective witness, it is your overcoming power, and it helps you to stand against the forces of the enemy that is launched against you.

Why Is It Necessary to Speak in Unknown Tongues?

I have always found this to be a very interesting topic because so many people have varying opinions. In Mark 16:17 (KJV), Jesus Himself says, "'And these signs shall follow them that believe, in my name, shall they cast out devils, *they shall speak with new tongues.*'" In the New Living Bible Paraphrased, that same verse reads, "'And those who believe shall use my authority to cast out demons, and they shall speak with new languages.'" Strong's Strongest Concordance in the Greek defines "tongues" (*Glossa*) to mean languages or the supernatural gift of tongues.

Tongues are our heavenly language given to us by God. The first time we actually see evidence of this supernatural event taking place is found in Acts 2:4: "And they were all filled with the Holy Ghost and began to speak with other tongues, as the Spirit gave them utterance." To simplify what is being said, you can interpret that scripture to say, "And everyone present was filled with the Holy Ghost and began speaking in languages they didn't know, for the Holy Ghost gave them this ability." So, contrary to what others say, think, or feel, tongues are not just gibberish or nonsense. It is another way for us to communicate with God the Father.

Romans 8:26 lets us know also that there will be times when you won't know what to pray. It is during these times the Holy Ghost prays through you in your heavenly language known as tongues. The scripture reads, "Likewise, the Spirit also helpeth our infirmities: for we know not what we should pray as we ought; but the Spirit itself maketh intercession for us with groaning which cannot be uttered."

Once you get filled with the Holy Ghost, ask God for a daily refilling. This is important. If you have a container of iced water in your refrigerator, and you pour out of that water every day without ever refilling it, the container will eventually become empty. It's the same thing with your spirit. If you don't seek a refilling from God and are constantly pouring out, sharing the Word with others, and so on, you will become empty. Once your spirit is empty, Satan can begin to fill your thoughts with sinful things, and you position yourself to become a vessel that he can use. But if we are full of God's Holy Spirit, nothing else can enter.

Sadly enough, you will find that even in this day and time, as prevalent as the Holy Ghost is to the church, there are still many pastors who do not teach about the infilling of the Holy Ghost or about speaking in tongues. They believe that it is a thing of the past. But all of God's Word is true and needful.

Without the infilling of the Holy Ghost, you cannot be a faithful witness, and you are operating with very limited power.

You are consuming a lot of information at this time. I don't want you to get bored or begin to feel overwhelmed. So, if you are feeling tired or starting to get a bit confused, it's okay to put down the book for a while and pick it back up tomorrow. You don't want to get frustrated. If there's something you need clarified, write it down so that you can check with your local pastor. I continue to emphasize throughout this book to be sure you have your Bible handy so you can see what I am teaching lines up with the Word of God. Don't take my word or anyone else's when it comes to your eternal being. You want to be sure that you are absolutely rooted and grounded in truth.

Who Is the Holy Spirit/Holy Ghost?

Elohem. One God, three manifestations: God the Father in creation, Jesus the Son in redemption, and the Holy Ghost in the church. The Holy Ghost is the power by which believers come to Christ and see with new eyes of faith. He has been described as the Comforter.

The Holy Ghost appears in the gospel of John as the power by which Christians are brought to faith and helped to understand their walk with God. He brings a person to new birth: "That which is born of the flesh is flesh, and that which is born of the Spirit is Spirit" (John 3:6). The Holy Spirit is the helper Jesus promised would come after His ascension. The Holy Spirit illuminates Christ's teaching and also works in the lives of individual believers in the church.

In Paul's letters to Corinth, Christian liberty stems from the work of the Holy Spirit, "Where the Spirit of the Lord is, there is liberty" (II Corinthians 3:17).

The Holy Spirit inspired Jesus with wisdom, understanding, counsel, might, knowledge, fear of the Lord, righteousness, and faithfulness. Thus, we come full circle to the New Testament, where Jesus claims the fulfilling of this prophecy in Himself (Isaiah 61:1–2; Luke 4:18–19 KJV).

Lastly, Isaiah 42:1–9 clearly summarizes the redeeming work of the Spirit in the saving of the lost. God spoke through Isaiah the prophet, saying, "Behold, My servant, whom I uphold, My elect One in whom My soul delights! I have put My Spirit upon Him; He will bring forth justice unto the Gentiles."

— I'm Saved, Now What? —

I am sure your local pastor will do a more in-depth study on the infilling of the Holy Ghost/Holy Spirit. If not, feel free to ask him or her any questions you may have. I know they will be happy to assist you.

Why Is Water Baptism Necessary?

First of all, baptism is an emersion in the water. It is an act of obedience, commitment, and a proclamation of your faith. Romans 6:4–6 identifies baptism with the believer's death (and burial) to sin and resurrection to new, as well as death and resurrection of Christ. It symbolizes the death, burial, and resurrection of our Lord Jesus Christ. Jesus would never tell us to do something that He would not do Himself. John 3:5 reads, "Unless one is born of water and the Spirit, he cannot enter the kingdom of God."

Some believe that baptism in the New Testament serves the exact same purpose as circumcision in the Old Testament. In the Old Testament, the act of circumcision was the symbolic cutting away of sin and a change of heart. This is found in Deuteronomy 10:16 and also in Ezekiel 44:7–9. In the New Testament, baptism depicts a washing away of sin (Acts 2:38; Titus 3:5). It is my opinion that Colossians 2:11–12 brings the two together. It states, "In Him [Christ] you were also circumcised with the circumcision made without hands, by putting off the body of the sins of the flesh, by the circumcision of Christ, buried with Him in baptism in which you were also raised with Him through faith in the working of God who raised Him from the dead."

Many believers are baptized in the name of the Father, Son, and Holy Ghost. They use the scripture found in Matthew 28:19, where Jesus says, "'Go ye therefore and teach all nations, baptizing them in the Name of the Father and of the Son and of the Holy Ghost.'" God and Jesus are One. He is God in creation, Son in redemption, and Holy Ghost in the Church. God is a title. Son is a title, and Holy Ghost is a title. Each one manifests itself in a different way, but they are still One.

Acts 2:38, "Then Peter said unto them, 'Repent and be baptized everyone of you in the name of Jesus Christ for the remission of sins, and ye shall receive the gift of the Holy Ghost.'" The Word of God tells us out of the mouth of two or three witnesses, let His Word be established.

- Colossians 3:17: "And whatsoever you do in word or deed, do all in the *name* of Jesus."
- John 1:1: "In the beginning was the word, and the word was with God and the word was God."
- John 1:14: "And the Word was made flesh and dwelt among us."

John used language with special meaning for both the Greek and Jewish readers. In the Greek, "word" (*logos*) was a key tern often referring to the power of reason for all creation. For Jews, "word" also had a great significance. They knew that God spoke His Word to create the world and to transform His people. Why do you think Jesus was called the Word? On little girl answered it perfectly. She said, "Jesus is all God wanted to say to us."

Baptism does not cause an inward change. It is an outward indication of the inner change, which has already occurred in a person's life. For further reading on baptism, please see the following scriptures:

- As administered by John: Matthew 3:5–12; John 3:23; Acts 13:24; 19:4
- Sanctioned by Christ's submission to it: Matthew 3:13–15; Luke 3:21
- Adopted by Christ: John 3:22, 4:1–2
- Appointed an ordinance of the Christian church: Matthew 28:19–20; Mark 16:15–16
- To be administered in the name of Jesus: Acts 2:38
- Water, the outward and visible signs: Acts 8:36, 10:47
- Remission of sins signified by baptism: Acts 2:23; 22:16
- Unity of the church affected by: I Corinthians 12:13; Galatians 3:27–28
- There is but one baptism: Ephesians 4:5
- Faith necessary: Acts 8:37, 18:8
- Repentance necessary: Matthew 3:6

Why Is Forgiveness so Important?

The ministry of Jesus Christ is built on total forgiveness. The first and greatest example of all is when Jesus was crucified, hanging on the cross after he had been beaten all night long and taken from judgment hall to judgment hall. With his rasping breath, he uttered the most powerful words ever spoken by any human being, words that ring from generation to generation. Words that were heartfelt from the body of a dying man, whose heart was broken, "Father, *forgive them*, for they know not what they do.'"

Forgiveness is the act of excusing or pardoning another for wrongs they have done. When we forgive, we pardon, remit, cancel out, abandon, tolerate, forsake, put away, omit what others have done to us. That's what Jesus did for us when He took on our sins and paid our sin debt. That is what we must do in order to be like Him.

If you are human, someone in your life has done you wrong, with or without a cause. You probably feel like they need to be punished. Forgiveness is probably the last thing on your mind. But, if you flip that around, you have done wrong to someone in your life as well, with or without a cause, and someone probably feels that you need to be punished as well. In order for you to flow as a true Christian, you must have a forgiving heart. Jesus tells us in John 13:15, "'The example that I have set for you, walk ye therefore in it.'"

If you are a new convert, you will find that the Bible is the only book that teaches about God's complete forgiveness of sins (Psalm 51:1; Isaiah 38:17; Hebrews 10:17). He is a God of grace and pardon (Nehemiah 9:17; Daniel 9:9).

For God to forgive sin, two conditions were necessary: (1) a life must be taken as a substitute for that of the sinner (Leviticus 17:11, 14; Hebrews 9:22), and (2) the sinner must come to God's sacrifice in the spirit of repentance and faith (Mark 1:4; Acts 10:43; James 5:15).

In the New Testament, forgiveness is directly linked to our Lord and Savior, Jesus Christ (Acts 5:31; Colossians 1:14), His sacrificial death on the cross (Romans 4:24), and His resurrection (II Corinthians 5:15). He was the ultimate perfect sacrifice, the spotless Lamb (Romans 8:3), the final and ultimate fulfillment of all Old Testament sacrifices (Hebrews 9:11, 10:18). Since Jesus bore the law's death penalty against sinners, (Galatians 3:10–13), those who trust in Him are freed from that penalty. By faith, sinners are forgiven and in other words, "justified."

God's forgiveness of us also demands that we do likewise and forgive others. Why? Because grace brings about that responsibility and obligation (Matthew 18:23–25; Luke 6:37). How often are we to forgive one another? Jesus placed no limits on it. He simply said, "'70 × 7'" (Matthew 18:22). A forgiving spirit shows that you are a true follower of the Lord Jesus Christ.

Chapter III:

Maintaining a Personal and Intimate Relationship with Jesus Christ

---

The effectual fervent prayer of a righteous man avails much! (James 5:16)

What Is Prayer?

Prayer is a two-way dialogue between you and God. It is your way of communicating with Him. It is a relationship, not a religious activity. Prayer is designed to adjust you to God, not adjust God to flowing in and through your life.

Prayer is an earnest, humble, sincere request to God, an utterance to God in praise, thanksgiving, confession. It is spiritual communication.

Types of Prayer:

- Adoration—Praise of God
- Communication—A desire to enter into a conscious and intimate relationship with God.
- Confession—Acknowledgment of disobedience.
- Intercession—Petition on behalf of another.
- Petition—A plea for personal help.
- Submission—Total surrender to God's will.

- Thanksgiving: Gratitude for God's grace, mercy and blessings.

As essential as prayer is in the lives of born-again believers, it appears to have been lost somewhere amid the yard sales, bake sales, recreational outings, backbiting, lying, gossiping, and only God knows what else. Peek into the majority of the churches today, and you will find that prayer has been gradually lost, along with the standards of holiness and the belief that Jesus Christ will soon come back for those who have made themselves ready. The house of God has become everything for everybody. No longer is it considered the, "'House of Prayer,'" as referred to by Jesus in Luke 19:46.

In order for you to grow and prosper in the Lord, you must pray without ceasing, have constant fellowship with the Father. Praying without ceasing does not mean that you walk around speaking in tongues 24/7 or saying thank you Jesus all day long. It means you keep your mind in a prayer posture. You meditate on the Word of God. In your quiet times, you fast, pray, and read your Bible to keep the devil at bay.

Lots of petty issues in the church could be eliminated if individuals spent more time consulting the Lord in prayer. You will often find that the petty issues have no truly significant bearing on your eternal well-being or salvation. Remember, without a proper prayer life, you will wither and die in the spirit.

If you give birth to a child, and from the time that child is born you spend no time with him or her, you don't feed the child, you don't communicate with the child, you leave it in the crib to cry day in and day out, eventually that child is going to die from starvation and lack of nurturance and care. It is the same thing with the new birth that took place in your life. If you do not feed and nurture it, it will wither up and die from starvation and lack of nurturance.

Prayer is one of your most powerful weapons. However, if you never use it, you will never know how effective it is. Without prayer, you will not make it.

Satan knows the power of prayer. So, his strategy is to present devices to keep you busy, out of the Word of God, and definitely out of prayer. I once read a tract from Chick Publications that showed Satan communicating with his demons. He said to them, "'Go after the weak Christians, because they don't have the power to cast you out.'" But his advice concerning those who were prayed up and dressed in the whole armor was, "'Stay away from the strong Christians, because they know they have the power to cast you out.'"

Now, if the devil is aware of prayer and that there is truly power in prayer and the Word of God, why don't the Christians know it? Simple. Satan has them too busy doing things to keep them out of the Word of God. By the end of the day, they are too tired to read their Bibles and pray. Don't get caught in that trap.

I was in a church once where the pastor was telling the people to "fake it" until they could "make it" and pretend like they were doing what they should. I was offended by this and asked him what would happen if Jesus came while they were faking it. Why not just teach them about holiness and total deliverance through Jesus Christ? Teach them how to pray and seek God. My advice to you, no matter who tells you to do something, if it is not found in the Word of God, don't do it!

I am sure you have heard this in your local church, but I feel compelled in my spirit to mention it to you again, "In a moment, in the twinkling of an eye" (I Corinthians 15:52), Jesus Christ is coming back. He said, "'I will come on thee as a thief, and thou shall not know what hour I will come upon thee'" (Revelation 3:3).

The Lord Himself admonishes us to "'Watch therefore, for you know neither the day nor the hour wherein the Son of Man comes'" (Matthew 25:13). God forbid that you are not ready when He comes. All the things that you thought mattered will mean nothing compared to what you will suffer if you are not ready at His ready or if you die and are not prepared. The choice is yours.

Why Do We Pray?

We pray because God never made prayer an option. His Word instructs us to pray and seek His face:
- I Chronicles 16:11
- Colossians 4:2
- I Thessalonians 5:17

We pray because of what God wants to do in and through our lives during prayer. We pray because we do not wrestle against flesh and blood but against principalities and powers, against rulers of the darkness of this world, against spiritual wickedness in high places.

Types of Prayer

If my people which are called by my name shall humble themselves and pray and seek my face and turn from their wicked ways; then will I hear from heaven and will forgive their sins, and will heal their land. (I Chronicles 7:14)

- Intercession: The act of interceding, mediation, pleading, or prayer on behalf of others (Romans 8:26: "But the Spirit itself makes intercession for us with groaning that can not be uttered … 27 because He makes intercession for the saints according to the will of God … 34 … it is Christ … who makes intercession for us").
- Petition: An earnest supplication or request to a superior or deity or to a person or group in authority (Psalm 20:5: "The Lord fulfill all thy petitions").
- Request: The act of asking for or expressing a desire for something; solicitation or petition; something wanted (Philippians 4:6: "Be careful for nothing, but in everything by prayer and supplication, with thanksgiving, let your request be made known unto God").
- Supplication: To ask humbly and earnestly, as by prayer; to make a humble request (Ephesians 6:18: "Praying always with all prayer in supplication in the Spirit"; I Timothy 2:1: "Supplication, prayers, intercessions of giving thanks be made for all men").
- Thanksgiving: The act of giving thanks; a formal, often public expression of thanks to God in the form of a prayer (Psalm 50:14: "Offer unto God thanksgiving"; Psalm 95:2: "Let us come before His face with thanksgiving").

- <u>Prayer of Faith</u>: Petition to change things. Always based on God's revealed Word. The prayer of faith never contains the word "if" (Matthew 21:22; Mark 11:24).
- Prayer of Consecration: Prayer to dedicate our lives to God. Willing to be used to go anywhere and do anything for the Kingdom's sake. Here we pray, "if" it be your will Lord (Luke 22:42; James 4:15).
- Giving of Thanks: To acknowledge fully in praise and worship (Romans 6:17; I Corinthians 15:57; I Timothy 1:12).
- Prayer of Invocation: To petition for help or support; to put into effect or operation. To call forth.

How Do I Pray?

You pray to the Father, in the name of Jesus. Jesus said, "'Whatsoever you pray to the Father in My name, I will grant it.'" I encourage each person—whether a new convert or a seasoned believer—to start each prayer asking God for forgiveness of all sins, known and unknown. Ask Him to cover with you the precious blood of the Lord Jesus Christ and to saturate you with His presence and His anointing. Ask Him to allow you assess into His holy presence, boldly as a priest and son, but humbly as a servant.

As you pray and study God's Word, you will find that the only thing that He honors is His Word. So, when you pray, give God back His Word. For example, when I pray for individual family members who may be unsaved or backslidden, this is how I pray, "Heavenly Father in the name of Jesus, I know that I cannot pray against a person's will, but you promised that if I delight myself in you, You would give me the desires of my heart. My heart's desire is to see my loved ones saved, so since their hearts are in your hands to turn as you please, give them a heart to serve you. You said in your Word that even though they profane your name in the midst of the heathen, not for their sakes, but for Your great name's sake, you would clean them up and give them a new heart and remove the stony places out of their hearts and give them a heart of flesh. So today, I am praying for restoration in Jesus's name."

This is why it is so important for you to learn God's Word through fasting, praying, and studying. The more you know it, the more you can you it. The more you use it, the more effective it becomes in your life!

Why It Is Important to Pray and Read Your Bible Every Day

II Timothy 2:15 (KJV) reads as follows, "Study to show thyself approved unto God, a workman that needeth not be ashamed, rightly dividing the word of truth."

As you study God's Word, you learn what it means. You gain knowledge about your Lord and Savior, Jesus Christ. You learn what is acceptable Christian conduct. You will find that serving God is not a lot of rigid rules and regulations dictated by man; it is a beautiful plan laid out by God to lead us into eternal life with Him. You will see the faith and strength of others who have gone on before you. You will learn of the weaknesses and failures of others and how true repentance restored them to God and allowed them to be used greatly in His service. And those who refused to repent were cast out of His presence. It is a defense when temptations come, because when the Word of God is engrained in your heart, mind, spirit, and soul, you are more able to resist the devil.

In the Living Paraphrased Bible, you will find I Corinthians 9:24–27 to be very clear and precise. In this text, the apostle Paul emphasizes a points that I believe is helpful to every Christian. He says, "In a race everyone runs, but one person gets first prize. So run your race to win. To win the contest, you must deny yourselves many things that would keep you from doing your best. An athlete goes to all this trouble just to win a blue ribbon or a silver cup, but we do it for a heavenly reward that never disappears. So I run straight to the goal with purpose in every step. I fight to win. I'm not just shadowboxing or playing around. Like an athlete, I punish my body, treating it roughly, training it to do what it should, not what it wants to. Otherwise, I fear that after enlisting others for the race, I myself might be declared unfit and ordered to stand aside." In other words, if you are going to be a Christian, live the life. Go all the way. Do what it takes to make it into the Kingdom of Heaven. Don't be a hypocrite and play church; anyone can do that.

—— I'm Saved, Now What? ——

There will be times when, as you read your Bible or pray, your mind will begin to drift to other things. The devil will bring negative thoughts to your mind. He will make you think that the Bible is a boring book of stories that do not apply to your life. He will tell you all that praying is not necessary. But as you continue on in Christ, you will learn that the scripture found in John 8:44 is very true. It stresses that Satan is a liar and the father of lies. He never comes to you with the truth.

You don't have to try to learn the entire Bible as soon as you get saved. An easy way to learn the Bible is to memorize at least one scripture a week. By doing this, you will have mastered at least fifty-two scriptures during the year.

I do encourage you to set up a special time each day when you can spend time reading your Bible and praying, whether it is early in the morning or just before you go to bed at night. I can tell you from my own experience that it is refreshing to be in the presence of the Lord. God has blessed me to wake up around 3:00 each morning. This is a great time for me, because it is time that is uninterrupted. There is no one ringing the doorbell, calling on the phone, or stopping by. It's quiet and peaceful, just Christ and me. It is in the still quiet moments like these that you will most often hear the voice of God speak to your heart and spirit. The Lord loves fellowshipping with His elect. And those who are used the most effectively are those who are most often found spending time at His feet, alone in His presence.

Be warned: it is so easy to get busy and put off spending time with God. Please do not get caught up in that strategy of Satan. It is for this reason I urge you to get up and put your time in with God early in the morning, even if it means going to bed an hour earlier and getting up an hour earlier.

The Word of God is not boring. When you begin to read it, you will literally see it come alive, and you will lose yourself in the pages! It will be good for you to have a dictionary and a concordance with you when you study to help you with words that may be unfamiliar. They are a good investment and goes a long way.

The more you read and study your Bible and pray, the stronger your relationship becomes with your Lord and Savior, Jesus Christ.

Separation from the World

In one of our many Bible studies, a new convert asked, "What's wrong with having friends who are not saved?" Their reasoning was, "All unsaved people are not bad just because they don't go to church." Remember what we talked about at the beginning of the manual: "Good morals don't get you to heaven, Jesus Christ does." This is one of the main strategies Satan uses to lure new and seasoned Christians out of God's will. I have seen it all too often. Satan, who is an enemy against God, will make you think that your pastor or leaders are trying to dictate who you can or can't talk to. You will think that you can handle being around nonbelievers. But I can assure you, in your flesh, you are no match against Satan.

As a pastor, I have seen too often in my own congregation individuals who were warned that they were walking "too close" to unsaved persons, and they took it lightly. Within a short span of time, these same individuals were back on drugs, alcohol, and tobacco. When they came back to church, their testimony was they don't know how it happened; it just did.

The Lord isn't telling you not to speak to unsaved people, because you go to school with them, work with them, live in this world with them, and you have to witness to them. But if you are saved and your best friend is not, what is your conversation going to be? In James 4:4 (KJV), we find the Word of God saying, "Know ye not that the friendship of the world is enmity with God? Whosoever therefore will be a friend of the world is the enemy of God." The Bible said it; I did not. II Corinthians 6:14–17 says, "Be ye not unequally yoked together with unbelievers, for what fellowship hath righteousness with unrighteousness? And what communion hath light with darkness? And what concord [agreement] hath Christ with Belial [Satan]? Or what part hath he that believeth with an infidel? And what agreement hath the temple of God with idols? For ye are the temple of the living God; As God hath said, 'I will dwell in them and walk in them and I will be their God and they shall be my people; *wherefore, come out from among them and be ye separate,'* said the Lord, *'and touch not the unclean thing and I will receive you.'*" So, once you give your life to Christ, you can't hang out with the same old crowd and do the same old things you used to do. You have to be a light that shines so that you can win the nonbelievers

—— I'm Saved, Now What? ——

to Christ. Remember earlier you read about being translated out of darkness into the kingdom of God's dear Son. It meant that you have been repositioned.

I Peter 2:9 is one of my favorite scriptures. If you are not sure who you are or to where you have been transitioned, this gives you a clear perspective. It eliminates all doubt of your Son ship. "But *you* are a Chosen Generation; a Royal Priesthood; a Holy Nation; a Peculiar People; that *you* should show forth the praises of *Him* who hath *called you* out of *darkness into His marvelous light.*" It doesn't matter what your status was before you were born again; this is what your status is now: (1) called out, (2) chosen, (3) royal priest, (4) holy, and (5) peculiar. You are definitely not the same. You have been repositioned!

God is serious about with whom we have fellowship. I Corinthians 10:21 was a real eye-opener for some, but it lets us know that God means business when He gives us instruction: "Ye cannot drink the cup of the Lord and the cup of devils; ye cannot be partakers of the Lord's table and of the table of devils." It doesn't get any clearer than that. So, you see why it is important to live a separate life from the world. If you have more questions, please talk with your local pastor or church leaders. I know they will be happy to explain in more detail the importance of surrounding yourself with true believers as you continue your spiritual growth in Christ Jesus.

Chapter IV:
Holiness—It's What God Requires

And a highway shall be there, and a way, and it shall be called the way of holiness, and the unclean shall not pass over it. (Isaiah 35:8)

Therefore hell hath enlarged herself, and opened her mouth without measure. (Isaiah 5:14)

Dr. Eason-Wellman is very instrumental to My Father's House Ministries, Inc. She is a tremendous help to me in so many ways, especially in the area of teaching. This particular chapter is from one of the many lessons she has put together for our Bible study. It was such a blessing to our ministry that I felt it should be shared with others and asked her permission to include it in this manual.

I am saved, now what? What is God requiring of me? God is requiring of you what He is requiring from us all: *holiness.*

What is "holiness"? Webster's defines it as the state of being holy or devoted entirely to the deity or the work of the deity. To the Christian believer, holiness is not just a religion; it is a way of life. Many people today question to need to be holy. It seems as if every one has a different perspective on the subject. When we instruct you to live holy lives, it is not because we want to restrict you from having fun. We are trying to keep you from going to hell. In fact, we are only doing what the Word of God has instructed and what God has always required.

- **Luke 1:74–75:** "That he would grant unto us, that we being delivered out of the hand of our enemies might serve him without fear, in *holiness* and *righteousness* before Him all the days of our lives."

Please understand, God requires that we live holy. It is not a process that you will pick up in a day or two. II Corinthians 7:1 says, "Having therefore these promises dearly beloved, let us cleanse ourselves from all filthiness of the flesh and spirit, perfecting 'holiness' in the fear of God." Holiness is something that has to be perfected. It is something that has to be practiced every day of your life.

Don't feel bad if after having been saved/born again for a week, you still have not gotten the grasp of holy living. In time, it will come naturally. The more you apply the attributes of Christ to your life, the better it gets.

- Ephesians 4:24: "And that ye put on the new man, which after God is created in righteousness and true holiness."
- Romans 6:19: "I speak after the manner of men because of the infirmity of your flesh; for as ye have yielded your members servants to uncleanness and to iniquity unto iniquity; even so now yield your members servants to righteousness unto holiness."

I recall reading in Leviticus 20:7, "'Sanctify yourselves therefore, and be ye holy, for I am the Lord your God.'" Our God is holy, and He requires us to be holy as well. Take a look at I Peter 1:15–16, "'But as He which hath called you is holy, so be *ye* holy, in all manner of conversation, because it is written be ye holy, for I am holy!'" In this passage, you see God giving a description of Himself. We are created in His image. We are to be like Him in all aspects of our lives. He said, "'For I am Holy!'" Therefore, if we are created in His Image, we are to be holy, too!

Note that our conversations have to be holy as well. This text refers not just to our speech; it is also refers to our entire lifestyle. How can we win the world to Christ if we are acting like them, talking like them, dressing like them? How can we show the world that we have made a change if we do not put off the deeds of the old man? How can we worship a holy God if we are not a holy people?

—— I'm Saved, Now What? ——

I John 3:8 says, "He that committed *sin is of the devil*; for the devil sinneth from the beginning. For this purpose the Son of God was manifested, that he might destroy the works of the devil." It is important for you to understand that two cannot walk together unless they are in agreement. God hates sin, but he loves the individual. If you live a holy life while you have breath in your body, you are guaranteed a life of eternity with Christ. However, if you choose not to walk with Him and to live in sin, you will live an eternity apart from Christ, in the lake that burns with fire and brimstone.

When Jesus comes back to claim His people, He is coming back for a people that looks just like Him. If you are still holding onto and participating in sinful acts of the world, you will miss His coming. Jesus is coming back for holy people. If you are not yet convinced, read the following passage found in Ephesians 5:27, "That He might present to Himself a glorious church, not having spot or wrinkle, or any such thing; but that is should be *holy* and without blemish."

It is our duty as Christians to practice living holy. Every day that you apply the principles of holiness to your life, you are one step closer to maturity. As long as you live on earth, you will have desires and urges, but God has equipped us to withstand temptation. He knows that we are unable to stand alone; that is why He sent His Holy Spirit to dwell inside of you.

One requirement of holiness is that you keep your body free from sinful acts. God now dwells in that temple in the form of the Holy Ghost, and He requires that you keep His dwelling place clean. You are not free to do whatever feels good. As a born-again believer, you have to learn to weigh the options of your actions and to count the cost. One of the reasons separation is necessary is if your friends are not born again, they are going to try to dissuade you from doing the things of God. They are not holy, and your holiness will show up the darkness in their lives and expose their unclean way of living. I Corinthians 3:16–17 says, "Know ye not that ye are the temple of God, and that the Spirit of God dwells in you? If any man defile the temple of God, him shall God destroy; for the temple of God is holy; which temple are you?"

It is not enough to say that you have accepted Jesus Christ as your Lord and Savior. You have to make a change. Your very character has to show that a change has taken place in your life. Some people make the confession that they have accepted Christ, but no one ever takes the time to explain the baptism of the Holy Spirit or the water baptism. All three are essential. When you receive Jesus in your heart for real, you will be eager to learn about every aspect of His character so that you can begin to apply the principles to your everyday life.

Being holy requires more than lip service; it requires *life* service. You have to submit your whole way of life to him. You have to truly let go of the wheel and put Christ into the driver's seat. When you ask the Lord to order your steps and direct your path, you can't go and try to work things out yourself. You no longer belong to you. You now belong to God. God does not expect us to fend for ourselves. He expects us to trust Him to take care of us.

Psalm 100:3 says, "Know ye not the LORD he is God, it is he that hath made us and not we ourselves. We are his people and the sheep of His pasture." You've made a very important decision in your life by accepting Jesus Christ as your Lord and Savior. In fact, it is the most important decision you will ever make. Don't be discouraged when life does not seem to be going the way you planned. There is so much beauty and joy in serving God. If you continue on in Him, you will reap the benefits not just of eternal life but a bountiful harvest here in this life as well. In your leisure time, read the following scriptures: Psalm 29:2: "Worship the Lord in the beauty of Holiness"; Psalm 30:4: "Give thanks at the remembrance of His Holiness"; Romans 6:22: "Ye have your fruit unto holiness"; and Luke 1:74–75: "Serve him without fear, in holiness."

In I Thessalonians 5:23, we see that God requires us to be, "blameless unto the coming of our Lord Jesus Christ." In Ephesians 1:4, He let us know that, "He had chosen us before the foundation of the earth to live holy." So, in retrospect, there is no way to escape God's great command.

As previously discussed, part of the process of living holy is found in Romans 12. It is in this chapter that God instructs us to present our bodies as living sacrifices, holy and acceptable unto God. Just as Jesus gave His life as a living sacrifice unto God for us, we should be willing to give our lives as living sacrifices to Him now.

You will not be able to reach this goal overnight, but with patience and endurance, you will grow into maturity and truth. Remember,

—— I'm Saved, Now What? ——

another name for the Holy Ghost is the Spirit of Truth, and once He comes in, He will indeed lead you into all truth. "Howbeit, when He, the Spirit of Truth is come He will guide you into all truth" (John 16:13).

If all this seems like too much information for you to take in at one time, remember the race is not given to the swift. You don't have to learn the entire Bible overnight. This is all about salvation. Learn to embrace each day as it comes. That's right: take one day at a time. God has called you to fight the good fight of faith. Trust Him to be your guide. When you feel temptation and you are not sure of your way of escape, call someone who is stronger than you are in the faith. Normally, they can offer words of encouragement and prayer to help you continue. Be sure to talk to your local pastor or church leaders with questions that you may have concerning any information you have read in this book.

Chapter V:
Questions Frequently Asked by New Converts

- **Is it really possible to live holy?** First, you must remember that God will never tell you to do something that you cannot do. His instructions are found in Leviticus 20:26, located in the Old Testament. It admonishes the children of God to live holy just as He is holy. Also, I Peter 1:15–16 says, "But as He which called you is Holy, so be ye holy in *all* manner of conversation: because it is written, 'be ye holy for I am *holy*.'"

- Jesus also reminds us that it is possible for us to live holy because, according to Romans 8:3, He came and fulfilled the righteous requirement of the law for us; for what we could not do in that we were weak through the flesh, God sent His Son Jesus, who *condemned* sin in the flesh. That simply means that He lived a holy life free from sin while He lived here on earth, never giving into temptations. That same Jesus now lives inside of you and me as the Comforter, giving us the power to overcome sin and temptation.

- **Is is hard to live holy?** The answer is no. But you have to have a mind that is made up to do so. Jesus declares in Matthew 11:30, "'My yoke is easy, and my burden is light.'" And King Solomon declares in Proverbs 13:15, "The ways of a transgressor [sinner] is hard." So, the Word of God clearly tells us it is easier to live holy than to sin!

- **What does the Bible say about holiness?** Hebrews 12:14 says, "Follow peace with all men and HOLINESS, without which no man shall see the Lord." So, you can't see the Lord without holiness!

- **What does it mean to present my body as a living sacrifice? I thought Jesus Christ had already died and became the sacrifice for us.** You are right! Jesus did become the sacrificial Lamb to redeem us from the curse of the law (Galatians 3:13–14). However, as Christians, we become partakers of His suffering, and it is our duty as <u>ambassadors</u> for Christ (II Corinthians 5:20: "Now are we ambassadors for Christ") to live a life of total surrender and self-denial. We must die to the things of the world in order for Christ to be seen in and through us (Galatians 2:20).

- **I hear people talk about tithe or tithing a lot in church. What does it mean to give a tithe or to tithe?** A tithe is 1/10 (one-tenth) of your salary (income), produce, or land given as a contribution to support a church or clergy. Please read the following support scriptures at your leisure: Leviticus 27:20; Deuteronomy 14:28; II Chronicles 31:5; Malachi 3:10–11; Matthew 23:23; and Luke 11:42.

- **Why do we tithe?** First and foremost, we tithe because the Lord Himself commanded us to do so. Malachi 3:8 asks, "Will a man rob God?" The Bible calls it robbery when you don't tithe. The Lord goes on to say that you are cursed with a curse when you don't give Him what is due to Him. He says to prove Him and see if He will not open the windows of Heaven and pour you out a blessing that you won't have room enough to store when you obey His command. But when you don't, He sends the devourer to destroy the fruit of your ground. It is best to obey God. I can speak from experience.

- **From what do I tithe?** The Bible tells us to tithe from all we possess (Luke 18:12: "I give tithe of all I possess").

I'm Saved, Now What?

- **What is the difference between tithing, offering, and giving alms?** Tithing is giving back to God a tenth of what belongs to him, offering is giving God a portion of what belongs to you, and alms is giving to someone who is less fortunate than you and who has nothing to give to you in return.

- **Why is it important to give?** Luke 6:38 tells us that when you give, it shall be, "given back to you good measure, pressed down, shaken together, running over, shall men give back into your bosom. For with the same measure that you give, it shall also be measured back to you." So, if you don't give anything, you can't get anything back.

Also, Malachi 3:11 says, "The Lord will *rebuke* the hand of the *devourer* for your sake."

II Corinthians 9:6 says, "But I say this, he which <u>sows sparingly</u> shall reap sparingly, and he which <u>sow bountifully</u> shall reap bountifully." Give a little, get a little. Give a lot, get a lot.

Galatians 6:7: "Be not deceived, God is not mocked. For whatsoever a man sows, that shall he also reap."

- **When I give my tithe, offering, and alms, what can I expect from the Lord?** You can expect so much from the Lord when you give. None of God's Word falls to the ground. Check out the following promises, and mind you this is just a few!
- He gives you the power to get wealth—Deuteronomy 8:18.
- He blesses you to find favor and promotes you—Psalm 75:60.
- He blesses whatever you put your hand to and causes it to prosper—Deuteronomy 7:28.
- He rebukes the hand of the devourer for your sake—Malachi 3:11.
- He makes your cup to run over—Psalm 23:5.

37

- He takes the wealth of sinners and lays it up for you—Proverbs 13:22.
- He supplies your every need—Philippians 4:19.

- **What if I make a mistake after I get saved?** I John 2:1–2 says, "My little children, these things I write unto you that you sin not. And if any man sin, we have an advocate with the Father, Jesus Christ the righteous. And He is the propitiation for our sins." So please note, there will be times when you will mess up and fall short of the glory of God. However, you must be careful that you don't get accustomed to or become comfortable practicing sin. When you sin or mess up, you feel a "dis-ease" (disease) in your spirit, and you want to get things right with God as quickly as possible. True repentance is having a godly sorrow that brings about an inward change that is reflected on the outside. You will know when you have truly repented, because when you see that same sin again, you will run away from it as fast as you can. You will not want to use that to breach your relationship with God again.

I mentioned *practicing sin*. That means when you make excuses to continue in sin while assuming that the grace of God will always be there. But Paul vehemently warns us in Romans 6:1–2, "Shall we continue in sin that grace may abound? God forbid! How shall we that are dead to sin live any longer there in? Know ye not that to whom you yield yourselves servants to obey, his servants you are to whom you obey?" So, one of my favorite questions to the church,: "Who yo' daddy is?" (Please pardon the grammar.)

- **What does the Bible say about the devil?** It lets us know that the devil is the archemeny of God and mankind. He is a being of supernatural power and some wisdom but is not omnipotent or omniscient. He tries to frustrate God's plans and purposes for human beings. His principal method of attack is temptation. His power is limited, and he can go

I'm Saved, Now What?

only as far as God permits. This evidence is found in Job 1:12. On judgment day, he will be cast into the lake of fire to remain there forever. Read Isaiah 14:12–20 and Ezekiel 28:12–19. These passages show that Satan was not created evil, but he rebelled against God when in a state of holiness and apparently led other angels into rebellion with him (Jude 1:6; II Peter 2:4).

The devil is the chief of fallen spirits, the grand adversary of God and man. Hostile to everything good. Basically evil. He causes spiritual blindness. Father of lies. Angel of the bottomless pit. Ruler of darkness. Deceiver of the whole world. There is nothing good in him.

• **Is hell real?** Yes! There are many references in the Old Testament and the New Testament. Many years ago, I was working a part-time job, and there was a guy who consistently asked me to go out with him. I refused him each time. I explained to him that in our faith, we did not date for entertainment, and I definitely was not interested in him being my husband. He started to slander the Christian faith and said that he was not convinced that hell was real, and religion and faith was a waste of time. I told him it was a matter of opinion. Then he asked me, "What makes you so sure hell is real?" I asked him, "What makes you so sure hell isn't real?" My answer to him was this, "I would rather believe that hell is real and find out that it is not than to believe that it is not and in the end find out that it is. Because if it is not real and I live like it is, I have lost nothing. But if it is real and I have lived like it is not, I have lost everything, because I don't get a chance to do it over after I am dead." So, my advice to new and seasoned converts alike is this: don't take a chance with your soul. You only have one, and this may be your last chance!

Not only is hell real, but the Bible lets us know that for those who are unfortunate enough to make that horrible place their abode, their five senses will be full intact. Read the parable of the rich man and Lazarus, found in Luke 16:19–31. In summary, they both ended up dying. The rich man went to hell, and Lazarus went to Abraham's bosom. (Remember, we talked about being the seed of Abraham.) In the verse 24, the rich man says, "'<u>Father Abraham, have mercy on me, and send Lazarus that he may dip the tip of his finger in water, and cool my tongue for I am tormented in this flame</u>.'" Verses 25 and 26 go on to explain how the rich man had lived a good life while he was on earth, and Lazarus had been tormented. Besides that, now there was a gulf that separated them, so even if he wanted to help him, he could not. You will be very much aware of what you are feeling in hell.

Revelation 20:11–15: "And I saw a great white throne, and him that sat on it, from whose face the earth and the heaven fled away; and there was found no place for them. And I saw the dead, small and great, stand before God; and the books were opened; and another book was opened, which is the book of life; and the dead were judged out of those things which were written in the books, according to their works. And the sea gave up the dead which were in it; and *death and hell delivered up the dead which were in them* and they were judged every man according to their works. And death and hell were cast into the lake of fire. This is the second death. And *whosoever was not found written in the book of life was cast into the lake of fire*."

- Revelation 21:1–2, 4, 8: "And I saw a new heaven and a new earth: for the first heaven and the first earth were passed away; and there was no more sea. And I John saw the holy city, New Jerusalem coming down from God out of heaven, prepared as a bride adorned for her husband. And God shall wipe away all tears from their eyes; and there shall be no more death, neither sorrow, nor crying, neither shall there by any more pain; for the former things are passed away. But the fearful, and unbelieving, and the abominable, and murderers, and whoremongers, and sorcerers, and idolaters and all liars *shall have their part in the lake which burneth with fire and brimstone*, which is the second death."

- **What does the Bible say about the return of Christ?**
  Matthew 24:36–39, 42, 44 read, "But of that day and hour knoweth no man, not the angels of heaven, but my Father only. But as the days of Noah were, so shall also the coming of the Son of man be. For as in the says that were before the flood they were eating and drinking, marrying and giving in marriage, until the day that Norah entered into the ark. And knew not until the flood came, and took them all away; so shall also the coming of the Son of man be. Watch therefore, for ye know not the hour your Lord doth come. Therefore, be ye also *ready*; for in such an hour as ye think not, the Son of man cometh!

I Corinthians 15:52: In a moment, in the twinkling of an eye, at the last trump; for the trumpet shall sound, and the dead shall be raised incorruptible, and we shall be changed!"

I Thessalonians 4:14-18: "For if we believe that Jesus died and rose again, even so them also which sleep in Jesus will God bring with him. For this we say unto you by the Word of the Lord, that we which are alive and remain unto the coming of the Lord shall not prevent them which are asleep. For the Lord himself shall descend from heaven with a shout, with the voice of the archangel, and with the trump of God and the dead in Christ shall rise first; then we which are alive and remain shall be caught up together with them in the clouds; to meet the lord in the air, and so shall we ever be with the LORD! Wherefore, comfort one another with these words!"

The Bible makes it very clear that Jesus is coming back! It is also very clear that Satan is a deceiver and that hell is real! The Lord Jesus is coming back for those who have accepted Him as their personal Lord and savior and have made a commitment to surrender their hearts and

Dr. Barbara Eason

lives completely to Him. He hath showed you what is good, and what does He require of you in return? That you do justly, love mercifully, and walk humbly with your God (Micah 6:8). Will you be ready when Jesus comes?

Definitions

A

- **Advocate**—A person who pleads another's cause.
- **Alms**—Charitable gifts to the poor or someone who has nothing to give in return.
- **Authority**—The power or right to give commands, enforce obedience, take action, or make final decisions.

B

- **Bond**—A binding or uniting force; a binding agreement or covenant.
- **Bountifully**—Given freely and graciously, generous, provided in abundance; plentiful.

C

- **Chief**—The head of a group or organization, person of highest authority, the most valuable or main part of something.
- **Compassion**—Sorrow for the sufferings or troubles of others.
- **Condemn**—To pass an adverse judgment on, disapprove of strongly; to declare too unfit for use or service.
- **Consecration**—To set apart as holy; make or declare sacred for religious use. To devote entirely; to dedicate.
- **Conversation**—The act or an instance of talking together.

- **Cornerstone**—The basic essential, most important part; foundation.
- **Courteous**—Polite and gracious, considerate toward others, well mannered.
- **Curse**—Any cause of evil or injury; profane, obscene.

D

- **Depart**—To go away from; to leave; to turn aside from.
- **Dispute**—Argument or debate.
- **Divided**—Separated into parts; disagreeing or differing in opinion.

E

- **Endeavor**—To make an earnest attempt to do something. To strive; to try to achieve.
- **Esteem**—To have great regard for; to value highly; to respect.

F

- **Foundation**—The base on which something rests; the supporting part, usually of concrete.

G

- **Give**—To make gifts or donations. Contributions; donate or bestow.

H

- **Harmony**—Peaceably or friendly relations; a state of agreement.
- **Holy**—Dedicated to religious use; belonging to or coming from God; consecrated.

I

- **Imperative**—Required.
- **Iniquity**—Lack of righteousness, wicked.

L

- **Lacking**—The fact or condition of not having enough.
- **Link**—A section of something resembling a chain; anything serving to connect or tie.

O

- **Obey**—To carry out instruction or order; to submit to the control of; to be obedient.
- **Observe**—To cling to; to adhere to; to follow; to keep or abide by; to take notice of.
- **Offering**—A gift or contribution.
- **Omnipresent**—Present in all places at all times.
- **Omniscient**—All-knowing.
- **Order**—An established method or system, as of conduct or action in meetings, worship, or court.
- **Overseer**—Supervisor.

P

- **Pastor**—Shepherd, minister of a congregation; a person in spiritual and jurisdictional charge of a church or congregation.
- **Peace**—Freedom from all disagreements or quarrels; harmony, concord. Calm, quiet, tranquility.
- **Present**—To give or offer freely.
- **Propitiation**—To cause to become favorably inclined, to win or regain the goodwill of; mercy seat.

R

- **Reap**—To gain or obtain a reward as a result of action, conduct, or work.
- **Redeem**—To buy back or make worthwhile.
- **Remember**—To bring back to mind; to keep in memory of.
- **Renew**—To begin again; to do or start over.
- **Reproach**—Shame, disgrace, or discredit.
- **Respect**—To feel or show honor or esteem; to treat with deference or dutiful regard.

- **Rock**—Anything like or suggesting strength or stability, firm.
- **Rule**—An authoritative regulation for action; conduct or method, and so on.

S

- **Sacrifice**—A selling or giving up of something at less than its supposed value.
- **Separate**—To set apart or single out.
- **Seal**—To confirm or authenticate by making a distinct mark.
- **Sow**—To plant seeds.
- **Sparingly**—To hardly give anything.
- **Stands**—To remain firm; unmovable.
- **Strategies**—Plots, plans, or devices of the enemy.
- **Strive**—To make great efforts or to try very hard.
- **Study**—To apply the mind to acquire knowledge.
- **Submit**—To give in to.

T

- **Tithe** —A tenth of what you have earned or acquired from your income, gifts, and so on, that rightfully belongs to God.
- **Tither**—One who pays tithes.

Closing Remarks

In closing, I trust that God has used Dr. Eason-Wellman and me to address some of the most common questions and concerns you have as a new convert. We did not want to overwhelm you with too much information, but we did want to give you enough to help you understand this awesome, life-changing experience you recently encountered.

We know that your local pastor and leaders will be there to give you one-on-one help as you continue this walk of faith. But we are always anxious to hear from our readers. So, if you have comments about the book or if you have questions that you would like to ask, here is how you can contact us:

Dr. Lahoma Eason-Wellman or Bishop Barbara D. Eason
My Father's House Ministries, Inc.
3323 Walmsley Boulevard
Richmond VA 23234

Lahoma2003@gmail.com or PastorBDEason@Hotmail.com

Our Web site is http://www.mfhm.org

We look forward to hearing from you. And just in case the Lord comes before we do hear from you, we hope to see you in the air!

God bless you!

Breinigsville, PA USA
03 August 2010

242945BV00001B/78/P